WHEN LOVE ISN'T FREE

A STORY OF LOVE LOST AND STRENGTH FOUND

ERNSIE FIDELIA

WHEN LOVE ISN'T FREE

*A STORY OF LOVE LOST
AND STRENGTH FOUND*

By Ernsie Fidelia

Copyright 2025 @Ernsie Fidelia

All rights reserved. No part of this book may be reproduced, stored, or transmitted by any means—whether auditory, graphic, mechanical, or electronic—without written permission of both publisher and author, except in the case of brief excerpts used in critical articles and reviews. Unauthorized reproduction of any part of this work is illegal and punishable by law.

Because of the dynamic nature of the Internet, any web addresses or links contained in this book may have changed since publication and may no longer be valid.

ISBN eBook: 979-8-9998412-0-9

ISBN Print Paperback: 979-8-9998412-6-1

Authentically written by a human. Pictures may have received a little AI help.

First edition published in 2025. Published in the United States by What s Holistic Health, LLC, Tampa, Florida

Disclaimer

This book is a work of personal reflection and creative expression. It is not intended as a factual record of any particular person, relationship, or event. Certain names, characters, places, and circumstances have been changed, combined, or fictionalized for privacy. Any resemblance to actual persons, living or dead, is entirely coincidental.

All draft drawings were originally created by an artist, and all poetry is the original work of the author. Select artwork has been digitally enhanced with the assistance of AI.

Table of Contents

Dedication viii
Acknowledgment ix
Prologue x
Introduction 1
Chapter 1: The Move That Changed Everything 5
Chapter 2: The Collapse 11
Chapter 3: The Losses Carried Alone 17
Chapter 4: Broken Trust 23
Chapter 5: The Day My Daughter Spoke the Truth 29
Chapter 6: Loss Within Loss 37
Chapter 7: My Reflection in a Broken Mirror 43
Chapter 8: The Night I Tried to End It ... 47
Chapter 9: The Lake Conversations 53
Chapter 10: The Hardest Room to Walk Into 59
Chapter 11: The Death of the Girl Who Lived for Him 65

Chapter 12: Becoming the Woman I Was Meant to Be..................71
Chapter 13: Forgiving Without Forgetting 75
Chapter 14: The Pain That Rebuilt My Soul 79
Chapter 15: Co-Parenting Through the Pain 85
Chapter 16: Rising from the Rubble 95
Chapter 17: For My Daughters 103
Chapter 18: Living Free 109
Chapter 19: The Gift 113
Chapter 20: Letting Go Without Looking Back 117
Chapter 21: When the Strong One Finally Breaks 121
Chapter 22: The Freedom in Acceptance 125
Chapter 23: A Letter to the Queen......131
Epilogue: Crowned in the Fire............137
About the Author..................141

Dedication

To every woman who has ever loved too deeply, lost herself in the process, and still found the courage to rise again.

This book is for the fighters, the survivors, the mothers, the sisters, the daughters who refuse to stay broken.

You are proof that even shattered pieces can be rebuilt into something beautiful.

Acknowledgment

First, I thank God—for carrying me when I could not carry myself. For every tear, every sleepless night, every moment I thought I would not make it...He turned my pain into purpose.

To my daughters—you are my reason, my why, my heartbeat. Every word on these pages carry your names because I never wanted my brokenness to become your story.

And to every woman who will hold this book in her hands—thank you. Thank you for daring to believe that healing is possible, that your story matters, and that your voice deserves to be heard.

Prologue

I did not come here to give you a fairytale. There is no white dress at the end of this story, no kiss that heals all wounds. I came here to tell you the truth—the kind of truth that leaves scars. The kind of truth that women like me carry in silence for years, until the silence becomes heavier than the pain itself.

This is not the story of a perfect woman with a perfect man in a perfect home.

This is the story of love turned poison, of trust cracked open, of faith shattered piece by piece until all I had left were my own hands to pick up the broken glass.

I used to think love would save me.

When Love Isn't Free

I thought if I gave enough, forgave enough, stayed enough—it would all balance out. But instead, love cost me pieces of myself I may never get back. There were nights I sat in the dark, face buried in my hands, whispering to God, "I can't do this anymore."

And maybe you've been there too. Maybe you've carried betrayal like a second skin. Maybe you've known the shame of silence, the rage of being unseen, the heartbreak of being left while still being "together."

This is my story—but it is not only mine. It belongs to every woman who has ever traded herself for the promise of love. Every woman who has bent so far she forgot where she ended and he began. Every woman who thought silence was strength, until it nearly destroyed her.

But hear me when I say this:
    It is also the story of rebirth.
    Of fire.

Ernsie Fidelia

> Of a woman finding her reflection again after the mirror was shattered.

Of choosing yourself—even when it feels like choosing death to the old you.

So no, this is not a fairytale. This is a survival story. A story of breaking wide open, and still daring to rise. A story of ashes, and the woman who learned to make them shine.

I have intentionally left blank pages before some of the chapters. Feel free to write your own notes, your favorite quotes or lines, or about the power you feel rising within you. It is part of the healing process.

Introduction

I didn't set out to write a book.

I set out to survive.

For so long, I carried my story in silence. I convinced myself no one would understand that my pain was mine alone, that speaking it out loud would only make me look weak. But over time I learned that silence doesn't heal. It hides. And what hides only festers.

This book was born out of that truth. Out of nights spent crying into pillows so my daughters wouldn't hear. Out of mornings where I forced myself to smile through exhaustion. Out of years where I poured into a man who had already emptied himself into someone else.

Ernsie Fidelia

It was born out of betrayal, heartbreak, and loss—but also out of strength, resilience, and the fire to begin again.
I wrote this book because I know I am not the only one. I know there are women everywhere who are carrying stories like mine: stories of loving too hard, giving too much, forgiving too often. Stories of being silenced, overlooked, betrayed, and left to pick up the pieces.

And too many of us have been told to keep quiet, to endure, to "be strong." But strength is not silence. Strength is speaking. Strength is surviving. Strength is choosing yourself when the world tells you to settle for less.

This book is for the woman who feels invisible. For the woman who wonders if she will ever be enough. For the woman who is tired of carrying the weight of love that hurts more than it heals. For the mother who is trying to protect her children while protecting her own heart. For the survivor who refuses to let betrayal be her ending.

When Love Isn't Free

Inside these pages, you will find pieces of my story—raw, unfiltered, and real. But I hope you also find pieces of yourself. Because while this is my truth, it is also our truth. The details may be different, but the ache is familiar. The silence is familiar. The longing is familiar.

And if you are holding this book in your hands, I want you to know something I once didn't believe:

> You are not alone.
> You are not weak.
> You are not broken beyond repair.

This is not just a story of heartbreak. It is a story of survival. Of fire. Of a woman who found her reflection again after the mirror was shattered.

And if I could rise from it, so can you. So come with me. Turn the page. And together, let's walk through the breaking—and into the healing.

Chapter 1: The Move That Changed Everything

In May of 2019, I closed the door on everything familiar and carried my life into Florida. To most people, it looked like progress—a family chasing opportunity. He had landed a new government job, and that made it sound like we were stepping into stability. Two little girls in the backseat of the car, bags of snacks in their laps, and me sitting in the passenger seat, trying to balance hope with fear.

But what no one saw was the sacrifice it took to leave. Georgia wasn't just a state. It was safety. It was family who checked in, friends who showed up, streets that carried memories of laughter and pain. Georgia was where I knew how to survive because I had roots. Leaving meant cutting those roots, carrying my children into soil I didn't know if we could grow in, and telling myself it would all be worth it.

I whispered that to myself the entire drive down I-75: This is worth it. This is for them. This is for us. It became a chant in my head, a fragile shield against the doubt creeping into my chest.

The drive itself was long and heavy. I tried to make it fun for the girls—pointing out billboards, playing music, passing them candy, and promising them new adventures once we arrived. They were too young to carry the weight of what was happening, and I didn't want them to. I told them Florida was going to be exciting, a new home, a new chapter. But deep down, I was whispering a different story to myself. One laced with fear: What if this isn't better? What if this doesn't fix anything? What if I just gave up everything for nothing?

When we finally arrived, the dream unraveled almost immediately. The neighborhood wasn't what I had imagined. Instead of safety and light, there were shadows stretching across the streets, stories written in the sidewalks that I didn't want my daughters to know. I had promised myself long ago that they would never grow up around certain environments—yet here we were, standing right in the middle of everything I swore I would protect them from.

The air was heavy. The walls felt thin. The silence carried more weight than comfort. I wanted to believe we had made the right decision, but in that moment, I knew something was off. My spirit wouldn't settle, no matter how much I told myself this was temporary. Still, I did what mothers do. I tried to build a home from nothing. I unpacked boxes with shaky hands but steady determination. I decorated walls that didn't feel like mine. I prayed in corners where fear crept in. I lit candles and whispered over rooms, asking God to cover us. I forced smiles I didn't feel so my daughters would believe everything was okay.

But the truth was, Florida already felt like loss. I lost the safety net of having family nearby, of having someone to lean on when I was exhausted. I lost the comfort of familiar streets, of people who knew my name. I lost the ease of knowing that if I crumbled, someone would be there to help me pick up the pieces. Here, it was just me. Carrying their joy in one hand and my unspoken fears in the other.

Every day was an act of endurance. Florida was supposed to be opportunity, but it became survival disguised as progress. I told myself over and over that it was just the beginning, that good had to come from all this sacrifice. I prayed constantly that the move meant more than what I could see in that moment. But deep down, I knew—this was not the blessing I imagined.

For three years, I lived in that tug-of-war between hope and reality. Shielding my daughters from the weight pressing in, while trying not to drown beneath it myself. Every laugh I gave them came with a silent tear I refused to let fall in front of them. Every prayer I prayed carried the plea, God, don't let this be for nothing.

Looking back now, I can see clearly what I couldn't admit then: Florida didn't just change my address. It changed me. It stripped me of illusions I had clung to. It forced me to face the truth about love, about sacrifice, and about survival. It became the doorway to heartbreak, betrayal, and lessons I never asked for— but it also became the ground where resilience was planted.

The move to Florida wasn't just about geography. It was the shift that set everything else in motion. It was the beginning of the unraveling, the moment when what I thought I wanted collided with the truth of what was waiting. The move to Florida didn't just change everything. It changed me.

Chapter 2: The Collapse

By late 2020, I could already feel it slipping. Whatever glue had been holding us together was wearing thin, and no matter how tightly I tried to hold the pieces in place, they kept falling apart in my hands. He was gone more than he was home. Always on the road, always somewhere else. At first, I told myself it was just work, just responsibility.

But as days turned into weeks, and weeks into months, I couldn't ignore the silence anymore. The silence was the loudest part. It filled the rooms at night when the girls were asleep. It pressed against me when I sat alone on the couch waiting for a door that didn't open. It tucked itself into my chest when I laid down in a bed that felt too cold, too wide, too empty.

Ernsie Fidelia

Silence became my unwanted companion, and with it came the sharp ache of loneliness.

I carried grief too—grief from losses no one saw. Miscarriages that weighed heavy on my body and spirit, reminders of what I carried but couldn't hold. I wanted to grieve properly, to cry and scream and collapse. But instead, I swallowed the pain and wiped my face because my daughters needed me. They needed laughter. They needed love. They needed to believe their world was safe, even when mine was breaking apart.

I told myself over and over that the distance was temporary. That when he came home, things would be different. That love would win if I held on tightly enough. But each return felt emptier than the last, like he was physically present but emotionally gone. And I was left carrying the weight of it all—the bills, the children, the house, the silence.

When Love Isn't Free

By June 2022, I thought maybe God had finally heard me. We moved into an apartment I had prayed for, a place I believed was our fresh start. I unpacked hope alongside the dishes and curtains, trying to fill the rooms with laughter, joy, and the promise of better days. I told myself this was the turning point, the moment everything would shift. I wanted so badly to believe it.

But just one month later, my world collapsed. The truth came crashing into the light, brutal and undeniable: he cheated. The betrayal cut deep, not only because of what he did, but because of what it meant. He let outsiders whisper poison into his ears. He let them tell him he was missing out, that family was a burden, that responsibility was a trap, and that he deserved more "fun." And he believed them. He chose them. He chose temporary thrills over the family that had loved him, supported him, and stood by him when the world didn't.

Ernsie Fidelia

It wasn't just that he betrayed me—he betrayed us. He betrayed the daughters who looked for him at night. He betrayed the sacrifices I had made, the roots I had ripped up, the hope I had carried into Florida.

The devastation gutted me. I cried until my body ached. I screamed prayers that echoed off the walls and bounced back into my own chest. I asked God why, over and over, knowing there would never be an answer that would make sense. I stood in the ruins of everything I thought we were building and realized I had been building alone.

That was my breaking point. The moment when every miscarriage, every silent night, every unanswered question, every lonely tear came crashing into one truth: I had given everything, and it still wasn't enough to keep him. I shattered in ways I didn't know a person could. I carried my daughters like lifelines, holding onto them as if they were the only pieces left of me that mattered. Because in many ways, they were.

June 2022 didn't just break my heart—it broke the version of me who begged to be chosen. It broke the illusion that love could survive without truth. It broke the silence I had worn like armor. This was the breaking point. The moment when everything I thought I knew collapsed. The moment I nearly lost myself. The moment that almost destroyed me.

But what I couldn't see then—what I would only learn later—is that sometimes it takes breaking to be rebuilt.

Empty cribs stood as silent witnesses, to the dreams I carried and lost. Yet in my grief, a faint light whispered—hope was not gone, only waiting.

Chapter 3: The Losses Carried Alone

My first miscarriage was in 2010.

It hurt, but I did not let myself feel it the way I should have. I told myself to be strong, to move forward, to pretend it did not cut me as deep as it did. At that time, I did not realize that unspoken grief can settle into your bones and wait there, patient, until it finds a way to come back up for air.

The second miscarriage was different. It was 2013, and that loss... it broke something in me.

I remember the day I found out like it happened this morning. It was a Friday. The doctor told me my baby no longer had a heartbeat. But instead of being able to remove the baby right away, I had to carry my child—lifeless—in my body for four more days. Four days of knowing. Four days of walking around with a smile that was not real. Four days of lying in bed, hand on my stomach, trying to pray, and finding only silence.

Tuesday finally came, and with it, the procedure. My partner never said much, but I could feel it—he blamed me. He did not have to use the words; it was in the way he looked at me, in the way his voice tightened. I started to blame myself too. What kind of mother loses her child twice? What was wrong with my body?

I was angry with God. I was angry with myself. And I was angry with him.

The grief did not just take my baby—it took pieces of my faith, my trust, and my joy. I started to withdraw, pulling myself into a shell because it felt safer there. I acted like everything was fine, but the truth was nothing was fine. The life we had before was gone. And so was the woman I had been.

Nobody around me knew the real damage. If I had not shut down emotionally, I do not think I would still be here today. But shutting down came with a cost—it froze me in a kind of half-life. I was alive, but I was not living.

Two years later, I got pregnant again. Instead of excitement, I felt fear every single day. I did not let myself dream about the baby, did not want to pick out names, did not let hope in too far. I was terrified of losing another child because I knew I could not survive a third time.

Then my body started breaking down. The pain became so bad that I went to the hospital, where the doctors told me I had a pinched nerve and could end up in a wheelchair. We were faced with the hardest decision of our lives: end the pregnancy or take the risk and go forward.

Ernsie Fidelia

We chose to take the risk.

That pregnancy was 39 weeks of fear, tears, and pain. My body hurt, my spirit hurt, and though he tried in his own way to be there, the damage from before had left a canyon between us. I carried resentment for the way he had blamed me years earlier, and I know now that resentment builds a wall even higher than grief.

But out of all that fear came my little bossy princess—a fighter from the moment she was born. And even though I did not know it then, she would be one of the reasons I eventually learned to fight for myself again.

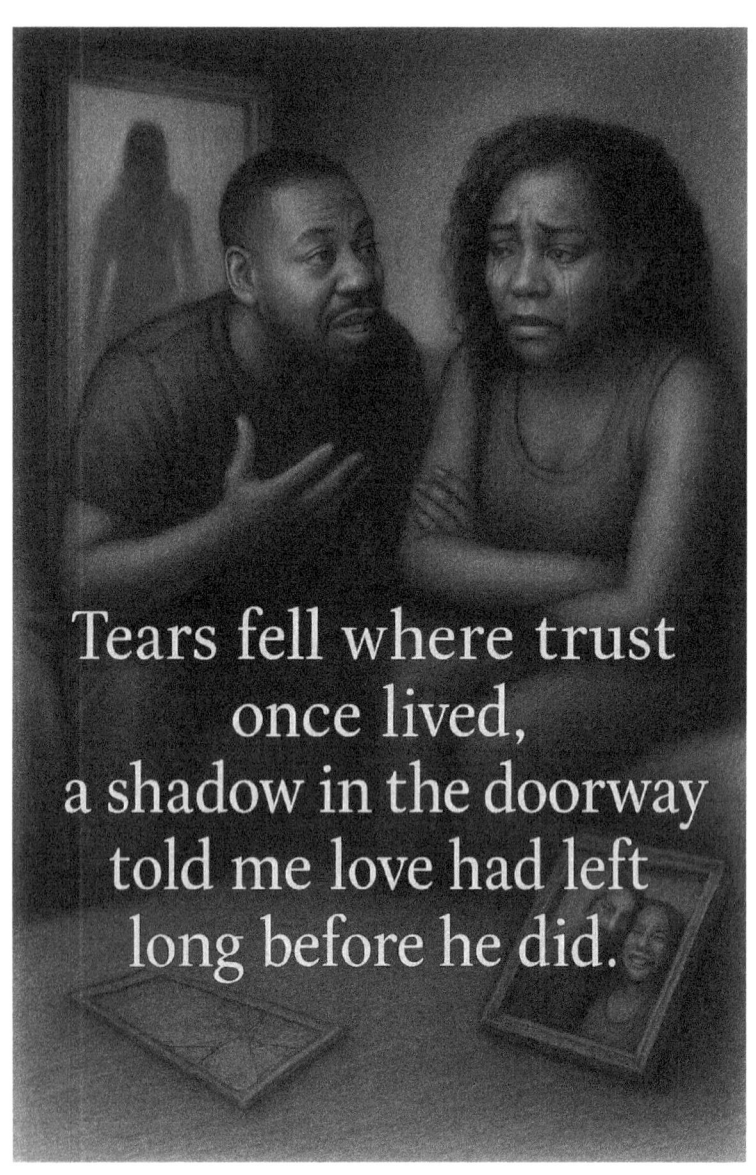

Chapter 4: Broken Trust

They say betrayal cuts deepest when it comes from the one who knows your scars. And that's why it shattered me so completely—because he knew my pain and still chose to weaponize it.

When those police lights flickered against my skin, I felt naked—not in body, but in spirit. Stripped of dignity. Stripped of safety. Stripped of the fragile belief that maybe, just maybe, he would never go that far.

The officers looked at me like I was dangerous, like I was some unstable woman who might harm the very children I had bled, fought, and prayed for. Do you know what that feels like? To be misjudged by strangers because of the lies of the man you gave your life to. I wanted to scream, *"Ask my children!"* They know I would never! I wanted to shout, *"Look at my heart—it beats for them!"*

But my voice was weak. My throat was raw from crying, from arguing, from being silenced too many times. All I could do was whisper, *"I live for my kids. I would never."*

And even as I said it, I could see doubt in their eyes.

He followed me like a shadow that would not let me breathe. His words were poison, dripping into ears that did not know me, into a system that too often believes the worst before the truth. He woke our youngest daughter, dragged her into the chaos, parading her innocence in the middle of my breaking point.

I was humiliated. Angry. Broken. But most of all, I was afraid. Not afraid of him—but afraid that his lies would stick. Afraid that one day my kids would look at me through his words and wonder if they were true. Afraid that his hatred would stain the love I had spent years pouring into them.

That night bled into the next day. And the next day, I found myself in the psych ward. Not because I was dangerous, but because I had to prove I wasn't. Imagine that—walking into a place built for healing, not because you were sick, but because someone you trusted painted you as broken.

The walls were white. Too white. The kind of white that swallows you whole and makes you feel like nothing. I sat on a narrow bed, clutching myself, and all I could think was: *How did I end up here? How did love bring me here?* Memories rushed me like waves. The miscarriages I grieved alone. The sacrifices I made—career, independence, stability—because I believed in us. The nights I begged him to see me, only to be met with silence.

And now this. This final betrayal that left me stripped and small. He told me he hated me. He told me he regretted our kids. He told me he regretted me. And sitting there, I almost believed it. But then, something rose inside me—a flicker of the woman I used to be. She reminded me: *Before him, you were whole. Before him, you had a name, a dream, a voice. And after him, you will again.*

I realized then that his lies didn't define me. His hatred didn't break me. His attempt to erase me didn't succeed.

>**Because here I am.**
>**Still breathing.**
>**Still loving my children.**
>**Still choosing myself.**

He made me nothing in his story. But in mine? I'm everything. And maybe that's what he feared the most—that even after all the lies, after all the attempts to tear me down, I would rise again. Not because of him. Not in spite of him. But simply because I am me.

Chapter 5: The Day My Daughter Spoke the Truth

There are betrayals you expect in life. Some you can almost see coming, like shadows crawling closer until they finally consume the light. But nothing—nothing—prepared me for the day my daughter became the one to expose the truth I had been too broken, too desperate, too hopeful to face.

I can still hear her voice, trembling but steady enough to slice through the illusions I had wrapped around myself like bandages on a wound too deep to heal.

He had been begging me. Begging me to forgive him. Begging me to believe that he was sorry. Begging me to let him back into the family he had shattered. His words dripped with regret, practiced and polished like he'd rehearsed them in the mirror. He told me he wanted us, wanted home, wanted redemption. And I—like a fool still clinging to the dream of forever—wanted to believe him.

Because when you give someone fourteen years of your life, when you share children, miscarriages, memories, and every ounce of your soul, you don't want to believe they're capable of throwing it all away so easily. You don't want to admit you built your life on shifting sand. So, you listen. You hope. You pray that maybe the nightmare is ending and the man you loved is finally waking up.

But my child—my baby girl—saw what I could not. She came to me with eyes too wise for her age, carrying a truth she should never have had to carry. She told me that while he was promising me a family, while he was asking me to trust him again, he had already introduced them to her.

When Love Isn't Free

On FaceTime.

The other woman—the one he swore didn't exist, the one he said meant nothing, the one he insisted was in my imagination—was suddenly a face on my children's screen. Their father, their protector, had dragged them into his betrayal, parading her in front of them while still lying to me.

In that moment, my heart wasn't just broken—it was ripped out of my chest, stomped on, and shattered into pieces too small to gather. I wanted to collapse. I wanted to scream. I wanted to erase what I had just heard. But her words wouldn't stop echoing: "Mom, you don't deserve this. It's okay to leave him."

Do you know what it feels like for your child to have to tell you that? To watch the innocence of her voice carry a truth meant for adults? It was rage. It was humiliation. It was grief so raw I thought it would kill me.

How dare he. How dare he place our children in the middle of his lies. How dare he let them meet her before even facing me with the truth. How dare he use their tender hearts as shields for his cowardice.

I cried until I thought my body would break. The sobs tore out of me like they had been buried in my bones for years, waiting for this moment to explode. My hands shook. My chest burned. I looked at my daughter, at her bravery, at her brokenness, and I hated him more than I have ever hated another human being in my life.

Not because he cheated. Not because he lied. Not even because he betrayed me again. But because he made our child the messenger of his filth. He forced her to be the one to pull the blindfold off my eyes. He turned her into the truth-teller when that was never her burden to carry. He made her grow up in an instant, while he kept acting like a boy.

When Love Isn't Free

I wanted to hurt him the way he hurt me. I wanted him to feel the weight of shame crushing his chest. I wanted him to wake up every day haunted by what he did to his family. But then—through the rage, through the humiliation, through the heartbreak—I realized something.

My daughter had just saved me. She gave me the strength I had been begging God to send. She looked at me in my brokenness and reminded me I was worthy of more than his half-truths and manipulations. She handed me the permission slip my heart had been too afraid to write: It's okay to let him go.

I thought about every sacrifice I made for him. Moving states. Leaving my career. Losing myself in the name of family. Carrying life in my womb only to lose it—twice. And still, none of it was enough for him.

And now? Now he dared to spit in the face of all that sacrifice by parading another woman before the children we made together. I hated him in that moment. I hated the way his choices burned holes through me. I hated how he made me question my worth. I hated how he forced our daughter to be braver than her father. And I knew—I could never go back.

Because love doesn't look like this. Love doesn't humiliate. Love doesn't drag your children into betrayal. Love doesn't ask for forgiveness while holding someone else's hand behind your back.

That night, as I rocked myself to sleep with swollen eyes and a hollow chest, I made a vow. Never again. Never again would I let him steal my dignity. Never again would I let him use my daughters as pawns in his selfish games. Never again would I trade my peace for his poison.

He thought introducing them to her would solidify his power. Instead, it solidified my resolve. Because when your child looks at you and says, "Mom, you don't deserve this," you believe her. You gather your broken pieces. You wipe your tears. And

When Love Isn't Free

you stand up. For yourself. For your daughters. For the love that will one day feel free again.

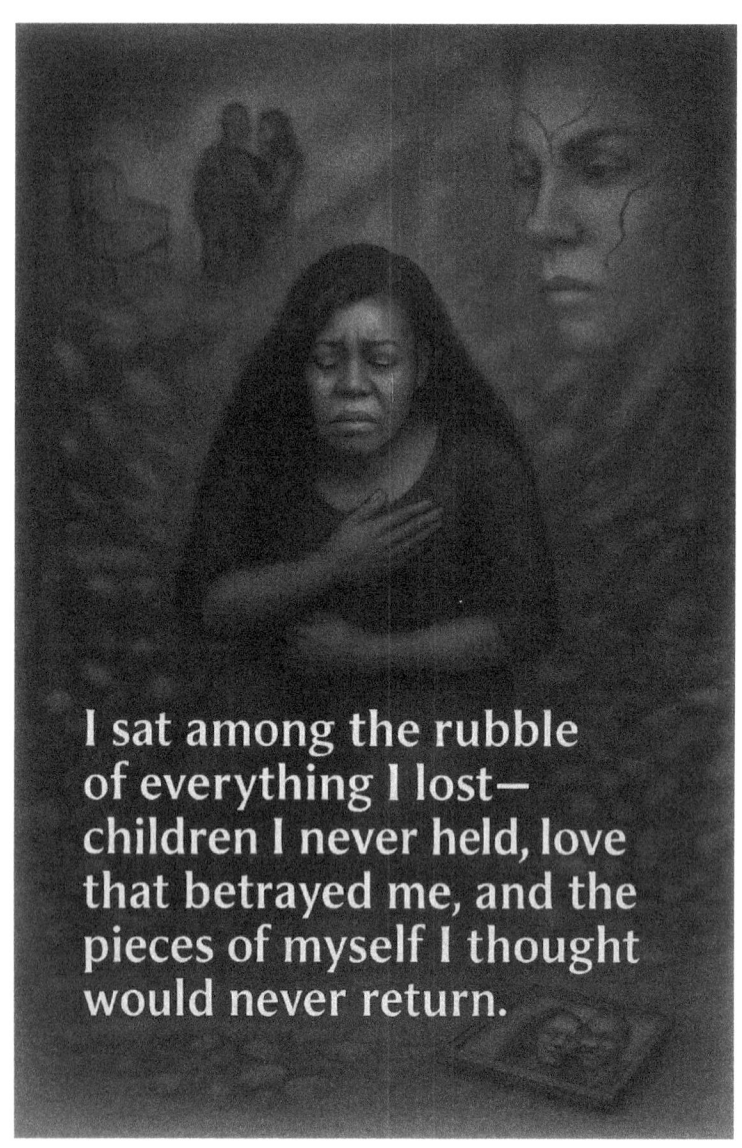

Chapter 6: Loss Within Loss

When a relationship begins to die, it doesn't always start with the moment you expect. It isn't always the discovery of betrayal, the sound of an argument echoing down the hall, or the slam of a door that refuses to close gently anymore. No—sometimes it begins long before. Sometimes it begins with the ghosts you never buried. The pain you refused to name. The grief you told yourself you didn't have time to feel.

Those are the ghosts that return when the house grows quiet, when your body is tired, when your spirit is too weary to keep pretending. For me, the cracks in our foundation were not just about him—not just about the lies, the distance, or the betrayal. The cracks were older than that. They lived in the wounds I never healed. The miscarriages that stole breath I never got back. The nights I wept quietly into my pillow, blaming myself, while he blamed me too.

The resentment that like a wall between us, built brick by brick, until neither of us could see over it. And the cruelest part? I thought I had moved past it. I convinced myself that if I could get up each morning, cook dinner, pack lunches, put on a smile for the children, then I must have been fine.

But grief doesn't disappear just because you refuse to face it. It lingers. It waits. And when life shakes again, when the ground beneath you begins to tremble, it surges back like a flood, demanding to be felt.

That summer, the water came over my head. The look in his eyes when he came home late. The way his voice lost its warmth when he spoke to me. The silence

When Love Isn't Free

that stretched between us until it felt louder than any scream. It all reminded me of those months after my second miscarriage—the silence, the distance, the way we stopped reaching for each other.

Back then, I pulled away because I didn't know how to grieve with him. I folded inward. I grieved in silence. And now, years later, he was the one withdrawing from me. And I realized the truth I had been avoiding: we had been drifting apart much longer than I wanted to admit. Loss within loss.

I had lost two children, but I had also lost myself. I had lost the version of me who still believed love could fix anything. I had lost the ease of the laughter we used to share. The way we once moved in sync, like two people who knew the other would always be there. The comfort of believing that no matter what storms came, we would weather them together. The truth I could no longer run from was this: we had both stopped fighting for each other a long time ago.

And that is the cruelest way love dies. Not with a dramatic ending, not with the bang of betrayal, but with the quiet unraveling. With the slow silence that builds between two people who once promised forever. With the way you stop reaching out, the way your words fade, the way your hands grow used to being empty.

It wasn't just him I lost. It wasn't just the children. It was the woman I used to be. The hopeful girl who believed family was enough. The woman who once believed love could save her. She was gone, buried under years of silence, buried under his distance, buried under my own pretending. Loss within loss.

I carried it all in my body. The heaviness in my chest. The tightness in my throat. The nights I couldn't sleep because the weight of what I hadn't said sat on my ribs like bricks. Grief became part of me. It lived in me like a shadow, showing up in the way I snapped at the kids, in the way I stared too long at the wall, in the way I avoided mirrors because I didn't recognize the woman looking back.

And yet—even in the drowning—something inside me stirred. A whisper, faint but insistent: You cannot stay here. You cannot keep living in this loss. You cannot keep giving away pieces of yourself until there is nothing left.

That whisper was the beginning. Not of healing yet—but of hope. The first spark of fire buried deep in the ashes. The reminder that even though loss within loss had nearly destroyed me, I still had a choice. I could face it. Or I could drown in it for good.

And though I was still broken, still grieving, still weighed down by everything I had lost, I chose to believe, even just a little, that I was not finished yet. Because loss within loss may have broken me—but it would not be the end of me.

Chapter 7: My Reflection in a Broken Mirror

There is something cruel about mirrors. They do not just show you your face—they show you everything you do not want to see. I used to stand in front of the mirror and see a woman who tried to keep it all together. Smiling when she was breaking. Loving when she was not being loved back. Holding on when everything inside her was begging her to let go.

But then the mirror began to shift. It did not reflect the woman I once knew. Instead, it showed me in pieces.

One shard showed the strong me—chin high, refusing to bow.

Another shard showed the broken me—
eyes swollen, tears falling.
Yet another shard showed the fading me—
the one who was losing herself, day by
day, trying to be enough for a man who
told me he could "do better."

I stared at those pieces, and for the first
time, I could not put them back together.
I did not know who I was anymore. Was I
the strong woman who fought for her
family?

Was I the broken woman who begged to
be chosen?

Or was I the fading shadow who stopped
believing she mattered?

That is what betrayal does. It does not
just hurt your heart—it changes the way
you see yourself. It turns mirrors into
weapons. Every glance feels like a
reminder of what you lost, of what you let
slip, of who you no longer recognize.

And yet...as much as I hated those reflections, I could not look away. Because buried in the cracks, I started to see the truth:

The woman I thought was gone—the one who was strong, bold, and unbreakable—was still there. Hidden. Waiting.

The mirror may have been broken, but it did not erase me. It revealed me. And, just maybe, the cracks were not meant to destroy me. They were meant to show me that even broken glass can still reflect light.

Chapter 8: The Night I Tried to End It

When I think back to that night, I do not just remember the pain. I remember the silence that wrapped itself around me, convincing me that no one would care if I disappeared. I remember the weight of loneliness so strong it felt like another body pressing down on my chest. But I also remember what came after.

I remember opening my eyes the next morning and realizing that pain had not won. That the same breath I thought I did not want was proof that I was still chosen to live. I was still called to be here, for reasons I did not yet understand.

Ernsie Fidelia

It was not instant healing. It was not a miracle where the sadness disappeared overnight. No—healing came slow, in small steps. It came in the moments I chose to keep showing up. For myself. For my daughters. For the woman I was becoming.

I began to understand that sometimes the darkest night is not meant to end you—it is meant to break you open. To strip away everything that is not true, everything that does not serve you, everything that was never love in the first place.

And from that breaking, you rebuild.

It took time to look in the mirror and see myself again. For so long, I only saw the girl who was not enough, the woman he did not choose, the mother who carried children that never took their first breath. But slowly, I began to see the fighter. The survivor. The woman who woke up from a night she was never supposed to survive.

When Love Isn't Free

If you are reading this and you have lived nights like mine—nights where the darkness feels louder than hope—I want you to know this: your survival is proof of your strength. Even if you woke up angry that you made it through, even if you are still carrying the pain, even if you do not yet see the purpose in your survival—you are still here.

And that means something.

It means there is more to your story. It means your existence still matters. It means you are needed in ways you cannot yet imagine.

That night I tried to end it became my turning point.

Not because the pain disappeared, but because I learned that my pain was not the end of me.

What I Learned That Night

1. Silence lies. The voice that tells you no one would miss you is a liar. The truth is, you are needed more than you know.

2. Pain does not mean purposeless. Sometimes your deepest wounds become the very testimony that saves someone else.

3. Healing is slow but possible. Do not expect overnight change—expect small steps. And celebrate them.

4. God does not waste survival. If He woke you up, it is because your story is not finished. There is still work for you to do.

I carry that night with me, not as shame, but as proof. Proof that even in my lowest moment, I was never truly abandoned. Proof that pain can bend you, but it does not have to break you. Proof that I can

When Love Isn't Free

walk through fire and still come out breathing.

And if I can, so can you.

Because the night you think is your ending can very well be the beginning of your becoming.

Chapter 9: The Lake Conversations

The lake saved me in ways no one will ever fully understand. It was not just water surrounded by grass and walking paths—it was the only place I could take off the mask. The only place I could stop pretending I was okay.

I did not go there to "get some fresh air" like people say. I went because inside the house, my chest felt tight, my thoughts were loud, and my tears had nowhere to go. Outside, by that lake, I could breathe—even if the air still felt heavy.

The first time I walked there after another late night of him not coming home until long after I had fallen asleep, I did not say a word. I just stared at the water, my reflection rippling in and out of focus. I thought about how fitting that was—I had become a blur, a woman I did not recognize, fading in and out of herself.

At first, I did not even try to pray. I was too angry at God. Too angry at myself. Too tired to package my pain into something polite enough for prayer. But then the words started spilling out—ugly, unfiltered, and louder than I meant.

"Why, God? Why me?"

"What did I do to deserve this?"

"Why wasn't I enough?"

The questions came like waves, one crashing into the next, and I did not care if anyone walking by heard me. I needed to hear myself say them out loud. I needed to stop swallowing my own pain just to keep the peace.

And then, one day, mid-yell, I broke. My voice cracked. My knees gave way. I sank to the ground with my face in my hands, sobbing in a way I had not allowed myself to in years. I was not just crying for him or for us—I was crying for every version of me I had abandoned to keep someone else comfortable.

That is when the realization hit me—clear as the water in front of me:

This is not about him anymore. This is about me.

It was never just his betrayal. It was the way I had betrayed myself repeatedly by shrinking, silencing, and sacrificing. By walking into the fire every day for someone else and pretending the smoke was not choking me.

That day, the lake became more than an escape. It became a mirror. Every lap I walked, I saw pieces of myself that I thought were gone—the girl who dreamed, the woman who fought, the mother who wanted to show her daughters what strength really looked like.

And with each prayer—even the angry ones—I started to feel God's silence differently. Maybe He had not been ignoring me. Maybe He was waiting for me to see what He had been trying to show me all along:

> **You are still here.**

Three words. Simple. But they broke something open inside me.

I left the lake that day still tear-stained, but I walked away knowing this: I had survived everything life had thrown at me so far. And if I had survived this much, I could survive letting go of him.

Chapter 10: The Hardest Room to Walk Into

The waiting room was too quiet. It felt like every tick of the clock was mocking me, reminding me that I was here, sitting in a space I never thought I'd need. Therapy. Just the word made my throat tighten. I had always been the strong one. The one who held it all together when everything else was falling apart. And now, here I was, staring at the door to the hardest room I'd ever walk into.

I wasn't afraid of the therapist. I was afraid of myself. Afraid of what might come spilling out if I opened my mouth. Afraid of admitting just how broken I had become. Afraid of putting words to wounds I had carried in silence.

When I finally stepped inside, the air felt heavier. The chair across from her looked too soft, like it was made for someone who deserved comfort, not me. I sat down anyway, my hands twisting in my lap, my chest tight, my heart pounding so loud I swore she could hear it.

The first question was simple. "How are you feeling today?"

I wanted to laugh. Or scream. Or run. How was I feeling? I was feeling everything. Broken. Betrayed. Humiliated. Angry. Numb. Exhausted. I wanted to say all of that, but instead, I just muttered, "I'm fine."

But "fine" cracked in my throat, and the tears betrayed me. One slipped down my cheek before I could catch it, and then another. Suddenly, the words I had swallowed for years began to claw their way out. I told her about the betrayal. About how the man I had loved for nearly half my life had looked

When Love Isn't Free

me in my face and lied, then turned around and placed another woman in the space that belonged to me and my daughters.

I told her about the humiliation. About the nights I stayed awake, wondering what was wrong with me. About the mornings I had to plaster on a smile for my children while my insides were falling apart.

And then I told her about the rage. The pure, burning rage that kept me awake at night. The rage that made my chest feel like it would explode. The rage at him for breaking me. At her for existing in a place she should have never been. At myself—for staying, for believing, for letting my daughters see me fight for a man who had already chosen someone else.

The therapist didn't flinch. She just nodded, her eyes steady, like she could carry some of what I was unloading. And that broke me even more, because

I had never had anyone just sit with me in my pain without trying to fix it.

For the first time in a long time, I said the words out loud: "I don't know who I am without him." Silence filled the room. It was heavier than any argument I had ever had. Heavier than the night I tried to end it. Heavier than the betrayal itself. Because in that silence, I heard the truth.

I had built my entire identity around him—his love, his approval, his presence. And now that he was gone, I was left staring at the empty shell of myself, trying to figure out if there was anything worth saving.

The tears wouldn't stop. They soaked through the tissue until it disintegrated in my hand. I felt weak. Exposed. Vulnerable. And I hated every second of it. I wanted to be strong. I wanted to sit there and say, "I'm fine. I don't need him. I don't need anyone." But the truth was louder. I needed healing. I needed release. I needed to learn how to breathe again without the weight of his betrayal crushing my chest.

And so, I sat there. Not fixed. Not healed. Not whole. Just sitting in the chair, face wet with tears, heart aching, voice shaking. That's the hardest part about therapy. It's not the questions. It's not even the pain you bring into the room. It's the way the room holds a mirror up to your soul and forces you to sit with the version of yourself you've been running from.

That day, I didn't walk out lighter. I walked out raw. But raw meant real. And real meant I was finally beginning.

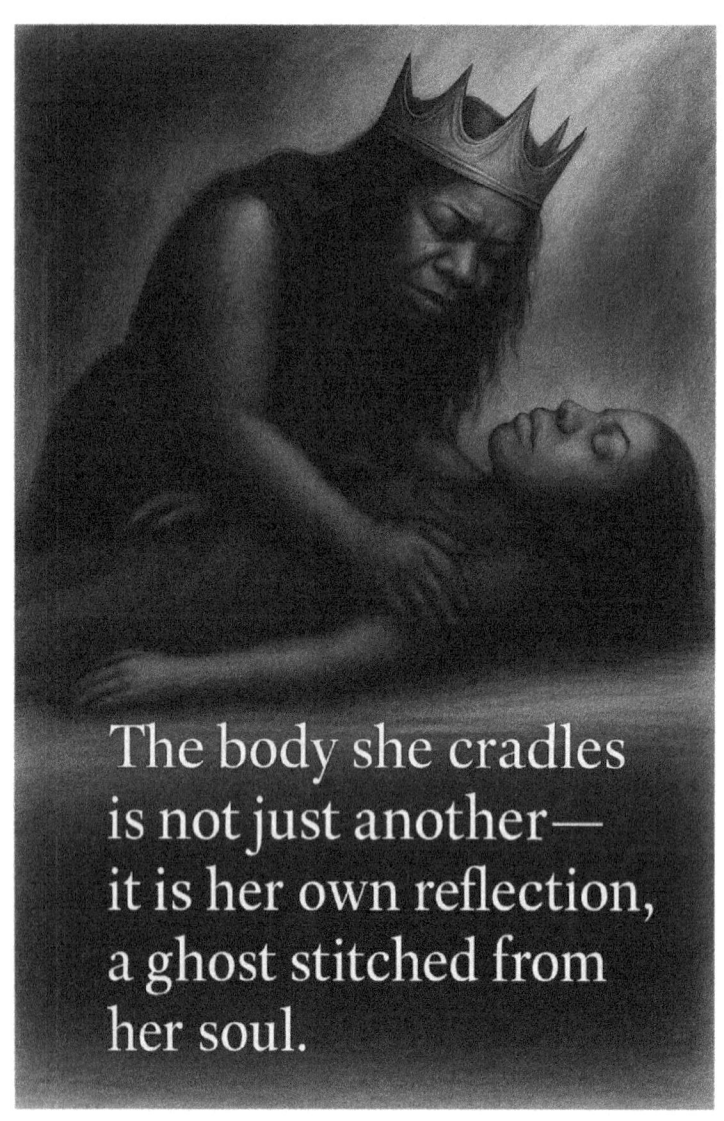

The body she cradles
is not just another—
it is her own reflection,
a ghost stitched from
her soul.

Chapter 11: The Death of the Girl Who Lived for Him

For years, my life was measured in him.

In his moods. In his silence. In his sighs at the end of the day. I built my world around his needs, as if my survival depended on his approval. What he wanted to eat. What kind of day he'd had. Whether he wanted space or attention, encouragement or quiet.

Every moment, every choice, every word was filtered through the question: What will he think? What will he want? I learned to read him like a book. I memorized the chapters, the way he slammed a door when anger was close, the way he dragged his feet when disappointment lingered, the way his laughter—rare and fleeting—was always a signal that I could breathe again.

Ernsie Fidelia

I learned him so well, I stopped knowing myself. I bent myself around him like clay in his hands. Shaping, shifting, softening. Making myself smaller, quieter, easier to handle. I smoothed my edges, hid my fire, dimmed my light so his wouldn't feel threatened. And in the process, I erased myself.

There was a time I thought that was love. I thought putting him ahead of me meant I was a good wife, a good woman. I thought being selfless was holy, that sacrifice was the price of keeping a family together. I thought if I loved him enough, served him enough, forgave him enough, he would never leave.

But love like that is dangerous. Because the moment they decide to go, they don't just walk out the door—they take you with them. And that's exactly what happened. When he started pulling away, when his eyes stopped meeting mine, when his body came home but his heart didn't, I realized I had no idea who I was without him.

The girl I had been before—bold, ambitious, full of light—was gone. Replaced by a shadow. A woman who lived only in his reflection. Who breathed only when he allowed it. Who smiled only when he made her feel worthy. And when that worth was taken away, I was left with nothing but emptiness.

It hit me one night. The girls were asleep down the hall, their soft breaths a rhythm of innocence I couldn't bear to disturb. The house was silent, but not peaceful. It was the kind of silence that hums in your bones, that reminds you you're alone even when someone is lying next to you. I sat there, staring at the walls, realizing I couldn't keep living like this. I couldn't keep living for him. Because living for him had killed me.

So I decided. The girl who lived for him had to die. Not because she was weak, but because she was done. Because she deserved to be reborn. Because she had given everything she had, and it was time for her to take herself back. Because she deserved more than existing in the background of her own life. That was the night I let her go. And even though it broke me, even though it left me sobbing on the floor, even though I felt like my chest was splitting open, it was also the

Ernsie Fidelia

first night I felt free.

Because the truth is—the girl who lived for him never really lived at all. She survived. She endured. She performed. But she never thrived. She never soared. She never tasted the fullness of life because she was too busy living for someone else. So yes, she had to die.

And from her ashes, a new woman rose.

A woman who chooses herself.

A woman who breathes on her own.

A woman who loves without losing.

A woman who will never again let her worth be determined by someone else's approval.

That night marked the end of her. But it was also the beginning of me.

Chapter 12: Becoming the Woman I Was Meant to Be

Let me be honest, killing the old me wasn't easy. She had been with me for years. She had survived heartbreak, loss, betrayal, and still somehow managed to keep going. She was strong in her own way… but she was also tired.

Bone-deep tired.

The old me was the girl who smiled when she wanted to cry. The woman who poured into others even when she was empty. The mother who carried the weight of the world on her shoulders because she thought asking for help made her weak.

She was a fighter, yes—but she was fighting the wrong battles. She was fighting to be loved by people who did not value her. Fighting to hold together a home that was already falling apart. Fighting to be accepted by a man who had already made up his mind. And the truth was... she was losing.

The old me could not take me where I needed to go. She had learned to survive, but I did not just want survival anymore— I wanted peace. I wanted freedom. I wanted joy that did not depend on someone else staying.

To get there, I had to bury her. I had to bury the people-pleaser who said yes when her soul was screaming no. I had to bury the woman who measured her worth by whether he came home at night. I had to bury the part of me that confused sacrifice with love, that thought enduring pain was proof of loyalty.

Because the truth is, the old me was built for a life I no longer wanted. And if I held onto her, I would never meet the woman I was meant to become. The new me would

When Love Isn't Free

speak her mind without fear of losing someone. She would protect her peace like her life depended on it—because it did. She would teach her daughters by example that love should never cost you yourself. The old me fought to be chosen.

The new me? She chooses herself. And that shift—that painful, necessary, soul shaking shift—is the reason I can finally breathe.

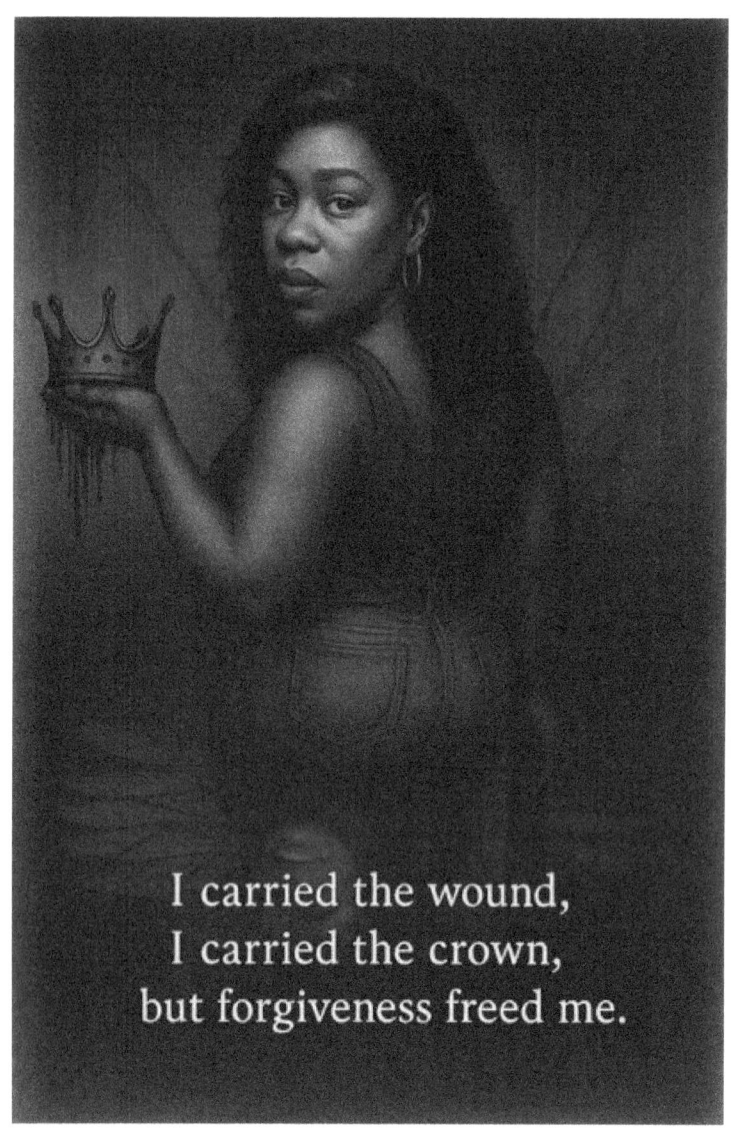

Chapter 13: Forgiving Without Forgetting

Becoming her taught me the hardest truth—that forgiveness is not for the one who broke me, it is for the woman I am becoming. I had to unclench my fists, let go of the bitterness that threatened to eat me alive.

But letting go did not mean erasing the pain. I still remember the nights I could not breathe, the lies that made me question my worth, the betrayal that hollowed me out. And I will always remember—because forgetting would mean I did not learn. Forgetting would mean I might walk blindly back into the same fire. But forgiving…that is where my freedom began.

Ernsie Fidelia

I forgive because I refuse to carry hate.
I forgive because my daughters deserve a mother whose heart is not poisoned by anger.

I forgive because I want to keep my soul soft, even after the world tried to harden it.

But forgiving does not mean trusting again.

Forgiving does not mean returning to what shattered me.

It means I carry the lesson, not the weight.

I forgive—but I do not forget.

And that balance, that quiet strength, is how I protect the woman I am still becoming.

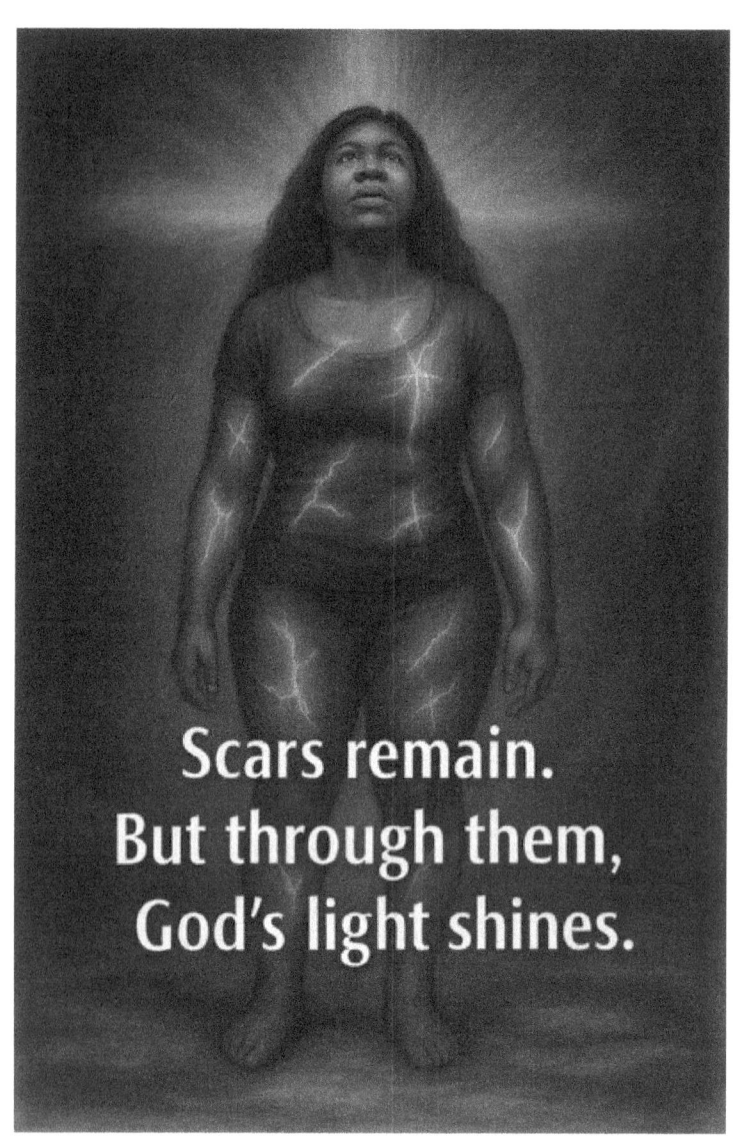

Chapter 14: The Pain That Rebuilt My Soul

I used to believe pain was punishment. That if I was hurting, it meant I had done something wrong. That if life was heavy, it was because I wasn't enough. For years, I carried that lie like a second skin, blaming myself for everything that fell apart.

But what I learned—through nights of tears, through betrayal, through silence that cut deeper than any words—is that pain is not always punishment. Sometimes pain is preparation. Sometimes it is the only fire hot enough to burn away the pieces of you that no longer serve who you are becoming.

When everything collapsed, I thought I was finished. The weight of betrayal pressed on me like a stone I couldn't move. My heart ached in places I didn't know existed. My body felt heavy with grief I couldn't name out loud. I moved through days in a fog, putting one foot in front of the other because I had to, not because I wanted to.

But even in that breaking, something quiet began to stir. At first, it was just survival. Getting up to feed my daughters when I wanted to stay in bed forever. Wiping their tears while mine fell silently. Pretending I was strong until, little by little, I realized pretending had become living. Pain stripped me down to nothing, and in that nothing, I found myself.

The woman I used to be? She begged to be chosen. She gave until there was nothing left for herself. She carried silence like armor, thinking it would protect her when really it was suffocating her. She thought love meant shrinking to fit someone else's comfort.

But pain buried her. And from her grave, I rose different. The woman I am now knows her worth is not up for negotiation. She knows her tears are not weakness but truth. She knows that survival is not the same as living—and she is done surviving alone. She is ready to live, loudly, unapologetically, fully.

I won't lie — it still hurts. Some nights the silence echoes, and some mornings I wake with the ache still in my chest. Healing doesn't erase the memories. It doesn't erase the miscarriages. It doesn't erase the way betrayal blindsided me. Healing doesn't mean the scars disappear. It means the scars stop defining you.

My scars are not shame. My scars are evidence. They prove I went to war with pain and still came back alive. They prove that what tried to kill me only revealed what was unkillable inside me. The pain rebuilt my soul piece by piece. It taught me to let go of illusions. It taught me to say no. It taught me to stop waiting for someone else to see my worth and to finally see it for myself. It taught me that silence was not my protection—my voice was.

I no longer ask to be chosen. I choose myself. The pain that nearly buried me became the ground where resilience grew. It became the fire that forged me into steel. It became the truth that set me free. And though it hurt—though it still hurts—I carry it now as proof. Proof that I am not what was done to me. Proof that I am not defined by who left me. Proof that even in the collapse, even in the silence, even in the bleeding, I was being remade. The pain rebuilt my soul.

And because of it, I will never be silent again.

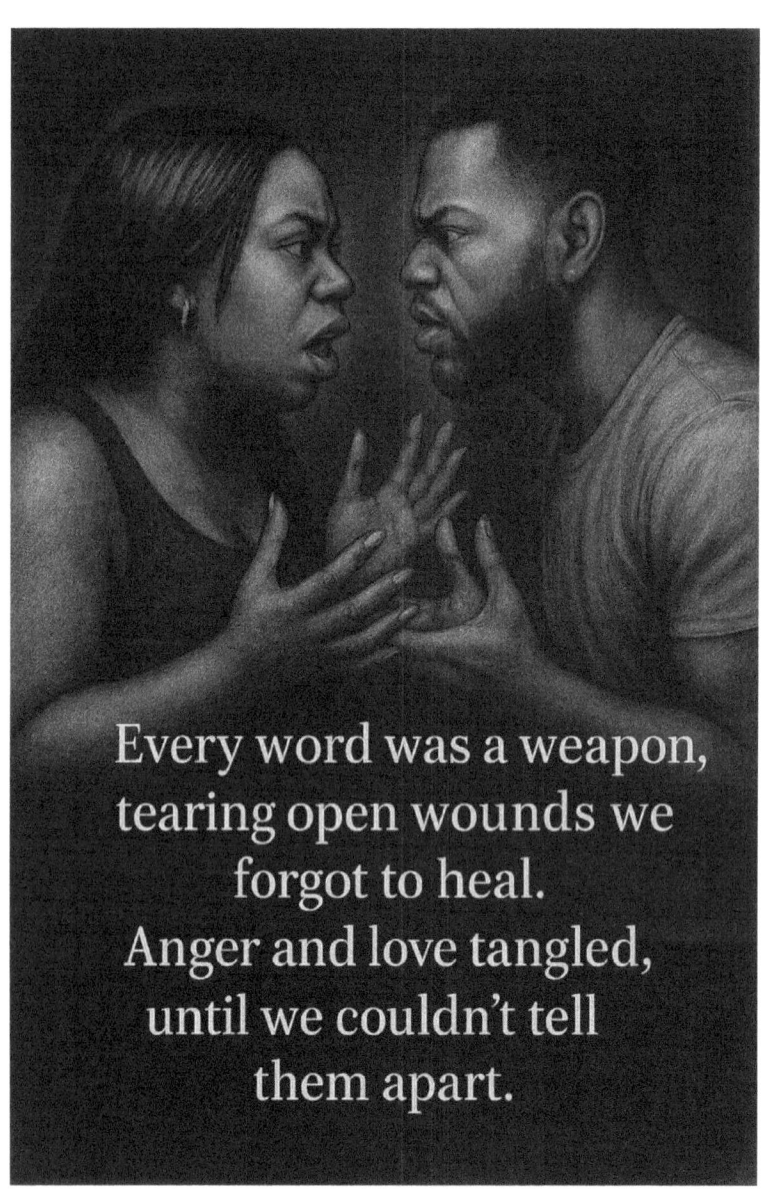

Chapter 15: Co-Parenting Through the Pain

Co-parenting was supposed to be about love—the kind of love that stretches beyond hurt, beyond separation, beyond betrayal. It was supposed to be about our daughters, about making sure they never questioned whether they were wanted, protected, or worthy.

But what happens when you're forced to co-parent with the very person who broke you? What happens when the man you once built a home with becomes the one you're constantly shielding your children from—not just his absence, but his choices, his manipulation, his inability to truly show up?

That's the war I lived.

The Illusion of Superman:
To my younger daughter, her daddy was still Superman. She saw him as strong, as magical, as the man who could fix anything with just his smile. And I let her believe it. Not because it was true, but because I wanted to protect her innocence. I wanted her to hold on to something I knew she would one day lose: the belief that her father could never hurt her.

The truth was uglier. He wasn't Superman. He wasn't even reliable. He had stopped supporting us financially long before he stopped pretending emotionally. I was the one paying the bills, putting food on the table, carrying the weight of school clothes, birthdays, field trips, and the everyday needs of two growing girls.

But I never told them that. I bit my tongue when they asked why Mommy was tired. I held back tears when they didn't understand why I couldn't always say "yes" to extras. Because how do you explain to a child that the man they love more than anything has stopped loving his role as a father enough to provide for them?

So, I carried the weight alone. And I let them believe.

His Battle for Control:
Even after everything, he still needed control. When he couldn't control me with love, he tried to control me with shame. When he couldn't provide stability, he tried to twist the narrative, so I looked unstable. Whenever I found even the smallest glimpse of peace—whether it was a smile on my face, a new friend, or the courage to start dating again—he tried to make me feel guilty.

"How can you move on so fast? What kind of mother dates when she has kids to raise?" Those words still sting, because they weren't about our children. They were about control. He didn't care that I had sacrificed my body, my dreams, and even my identity for over a decade to build him up. He only cared that I dared to build myself back without him.

It didn't matter that he had already chosen someone else. It didn't matter that he had introduced other women into their lives, even through a phone screen, before I had the chance to process our ending.

The double standard was clear: he could betray me, humiliate me, and destroy our home, but the
moment I took a breath of freedom, suddenly I was a "bad mother."

Protecting My Daughters from His Failures:
Co-parenting meant living in two realities. In one, I was the sole provider, making sure my daughters were cared for, loved, and stable. In the other, I was expected to pretend—to act like their father was still the man they could count on, even when he wasn't showing up.

When Love Isn't Free

My oldest daughter started to see through it. She was older, wiser, able to connect dots her little sister couldn't. She knew who was really there at night when the tears fell. She knew who was signing the school forms, packing the lunches, making sure the lights stayed on. And she hated watching me carry it alone.

I'll never forget the night she said, "Mom, you don't have to let him treat you like this. It's okay to walk away." Her words were both a knife and a bandage. A knife because they confirmed what I already knew—that our daughters were being pulled into a war they never asked to fight. But a bandage, because hearing her say it out loud gave me permission to finally believe it myself.

My heart shattered, knowing she had to grow up faster than she should have, but it also swelled with pride that she saw me, really saw me.

The Silent War of Co-Parenting:

Co-parenting with him was not about raising kids together—it was about surviving his attempts to make me doubt myself. It was the smirk he wore when I showed up tired but determined. It was the questions he planted in our daughters' heads to make them wonder if I was enough. It was his constant need to insert himself whenever I took even one step forward.

There were moments I hated him so much it scared me. Moments I wanted to scream until the neighbors heard every truth he tried to bury. Moments I wished I could cut him off completely, erase his name, and move on without ever looking back.

But I couldn't. Because my daughters love him. And because, as much as it kills me, children don't need to carry their parents' failures. So, I played the role. I bit my tongue. I swallowed my rage. I covered his absence with excuses that tasted like poison in my mouth. And every time I did,

I hated him more for making me protect his image instead of protecting my own peace.

Rising Anyway:
Co-parenting with a narcissist meant he tried to make me feel like I was losing—even when I was winning. But the truth is, I rose anyway. I may have been broken, humiliated, betrayed, and abandoned, but I kept standing. I kept showing up to school meetings, to doctor's appointments, to dance recitals. I kept loving my daughters through the confusion, through the lies, through the war he created.

And in the end, I realized this: He may try to control the story, but I am the one writing the ending.

Co-parenting was never about him. It was never about me. It was about two little girls who deserve to know what resilience looks like. Who deserve to see that no matter how deeply love can wound you,

you can still rise, still heal, and still become more.

And that's what I chose. Not for him. Not even for me. But for them.

Chapter 16: Rising from the Rubble

When everything falls apart, it does not happen neatly. It is messy. It is loud. It is painful. But when the dust finally settles, you are left staring at the rubble—pieces of a life you thought would last forever. That was me. Standing there, surrounded by the wreckage of my relationship, my trust, my identity.

At first, I did not know where to start. Do I pick up the pieces and try to rebuild what was lost? Or do I leave them there, a monument to everything I survived, and walk toward something new?

The old me would have tried to rebuild. She would have been on her knees, piecing it back together, even if the foundation were cracked beyond repair. But that woman...she was now gone. This time, I was not rebuilding for him. I was rebuilding for me.

It started small—getting out of bed when I did not feel like it, going for walks, writing down my thoughts instead of letting them eat me alive. I stopped wearing the mask of "I'm fine" and started allowing myself to feel. To grieve. To get angry. To let go. I began to see the rubble differently.

It was not just a reminder of what I lost— it was proof that I survived. Proof that even when everything collapsed, I was still standing. And that is when I realized something powerful. The version of me that was appearing from this wreckage was stronger, wiser, and freer than the woman who had been buried under it.

Every tear I had cried, every sleepless night, every moment I thought I could not go on—they had all been part of the process of building me back up. Not into the same shape I had been before, but into something entirely new.

I did not just rise from the rubble. I carried it with me as a reminder that I can survive the worst—and still become the best version of myself.

Finding yourself after losing everything—your confidence, your identity, your sense of worth—is not a straight line. It is messy, it is painful, and some days it will feel like you are moving backward. But I promise you, every small step you take counts.

The 7 Steps to Finding Yourself Again

These are the steps I took—the same ones I want to pass on to you, because I know what it feels like to wake up and not recognize the woman staring back at you.

Step 1: Face Yourself in the Mirror

Stop avoiding your own reflection. Look at yourself—really look. Not to critique, not to find flaws, but to see the woman who has survived everything life has thrown at her. Speak to her. Remind her she is worthy, strong, and enough, even if it feels like a lie at first.

This is where rebuilding begins—with honesty.

Step 2: Reclaim Your Voice
Silence can become a prison. Start speaking up—even in small ways. Say "no" when you mean it. Say "yes" when you feel it. Tell your truth out loud, even if your voice shakes. Every time you speak, you are teaching yourself that your voice matters.

Step 3: Break the Pattern of People-Pleasing
Stop trying to earn love by giving until there is nothing left of you. Love is not a payment plan. You do not have to shrink yourself to be worthy of staying. Every time you choose yourself without guilt, you are building a new habit—one rooted in self-respect.

Step 4: Create Sacred Time for Yourself

Healing needs space. Whether it is a walk by the lake, journaling at night, or sitting in silence with your coffee in the morning, make time that is yours alone. Do not explain it. Do not apologize for it. Protect it like your life depends on it—because in a way, it does.

Step 5: Let Yourself Feel Everything

Stop pushing your emotions down just to look strong. Cry when you need to. Scream into a pillow if you must. Sit with the sadness until it passes. The only way out of the pain is through it.

Step 6: Forgive—But Not to Forget

Forgiveness is a release, not an erasure. You forgive so you can set yourself free from the grip of resentment, but you remember the lesson, so you never repeat it.

Step 7: Choose Yourself Daily

This is not a one-time decision—it is a daily commitment. Some days you will do it with confidence; other days you will do it through tears. But you do it. You show up for yourself repeatedly until it becomes natural.

These steps are not magic. They will not erase the pain overnight. But they are the map I used to climb out of the place where I thought I would never find myself again.

And if you are reading this feeling like you are lost, I want you to know:

You are not gone. You are not broken beyond repair. You are still here.

Chapter 17: For My Daughters

To my daughters,

I need you to know that every choice I have made to heal was not just for me—it was for you.

I think about the day you might be standing where I once stood, holding onto someone who makes you feel small, questioning your worth because of how they treat you. I pray that day never comes. But if it does, I need you to remember what I am about to say.

You are not defined by who loves you or who walks away.

Ernsie Fidelia

You are not defined by the mistakes you have made or the seasons you have survived.

You are not defined by the pain someone else caused. You are enough. Just as you are.

When I stayed too long, when I accepted less than I deserved. It was not because I did not love you—it was because I did not yet know how to love myself. I thought I was protecting you by keeping the family together. I thought my silence was strength. But now I see that my silence was teaching you the wrong lesson.

I do not want you to inherit my patterns.

I do not want you to mistake endurance for love.

I do not want you to think you have to bleed to prove your worth.

I want you to know that real love does not dim your light—it helps you shine brighter.

When Love Isn't Free

Real love feels safe. Real love never makes you choose between your dignity and someone else's comfort.

And if you ever find yourself in a place where the walls feel like they are closing in…walk. Even if your voice shakes. Even if you do not know where you are going next. Walk, because you deserve to breathe.

I also want you to know that strength does not mean you never cry. Strength is letting the tears fall and getting up anyway. Strength is asking for help when you need it. Strength is choosing yourself even when it breaks your heart to do so.

The day I decided to heal, I was not just saving myself—I was breaking a cycle so you would never have to. I want you to see what it looks like when a woman refuses to disappear, when she rebuilds herself piece by piece until she becomes someone even she is proud of.

And if you ever forget, look at me. Look at

the woman I have become. Look at the way I love myself now. Look at the way I no longer apologize for existing. That is the gift I want to give you—not just in words, but in the life I live in front of you every day.

My prayer is that you will always know this:

You never have to pay the price of acceptance. The only acceptance you need is your own.

Chapter 18: Living Free

Freedom did not come in a single moment. It was not a door that swung wide open one day and suddenly I was out. No—freedom came piece by piece, choice by choice, day by day. For too long, I lived for him. For too long, I bent myself into shapes that I thought made him comfortable, while I suffocated in silence. I gave him my laughter, my time, my body, my dreams—and when he left me empty, I thought that meant I was not enough.

But the truth is, I was always enough. I just had to remember it. Living free meant learning to breathe again without asking permission. It meant walking into a room and not shrinking. It meant smiling without waiting for approval. Freedom looked like standing in the mirror, and instead of picking apart my flaws, I started to bless myself: "This body has carried children. This body has survived grief. This body is strong. This body is mine."

Living free meant putting boundaries where walls of pain used to be. It meant saying "no" without guilt, and "yes" to what made my spirit rise. It meant dancing in the kitchen with my daughters, our laughter echoing louder than the memories of arguments.

For the first time, I felt the wind on my skin and realized—this is mine. This moment. This breath. This life. And I refuse to waste it living for someone else. Living free does not mean I forgot what I lost. It means I finally understood what I gained. Strength. Peace. Self-respect. The courage to love myself with flaws and all.

I live free because I chose me. I live free because chains can only hold you if you refuse to break them. I live free because

When Love Isn't Free

God's purpose for me is greater than the pain I endured.

And now when I stretch my arms wide to the sky, it is not in desperation. It is in celebration.

I am free. Finally, beautifully, unapologetically free.

Chapter 19: The Gift

For so long, I thought love was something I had to beg for. I thought peace was something only other people deserved. I thought worth was something I had lost when he betrayed me, when I miscarried, when I broke. But what I did not know then is that the gift was already mine. The gift is love—not the kind that left me crying into a pillow, but the love I found when I looked in my daughters' eyes and realized I was still their safe place, even when I felt like I was falling apart.

It is the love I learned to give myself when I finally said, "You are enough, even if no one else says so." The gift is peace—not silence, not pretending, but the kind of peace that comes when you stop chasing people who do not know your value. It is the peace I found walking around that lake, hand on my chest, tears running down my face, finally telling God, "Take this pain before it kills me."

And in return—He gave me calm. The gift is worth—and I had to crawl through the rubble to see it. I had to bury the old me who thought I was too much, too broken, too hard to love. My worth survived every lie. It outlasted every betrayal. It lives in the scars I carry and in the way I rise anyway.

This gift—love, peace, worth— I almost lost it. I almost ended it all before I realized God never left me empty-handed. Even when I felt stripped bare, He pressed these gifts into my palms. Now I hold them close. I pass them to my daughters.

I write them into these pages so another woman sitting in her own darkness will know: The gift is already inside you. You do not have to earn it. You do not have to beg for it. You only must remember it. I thought betrayal took everything from

When Love Isn't Free

me. But now I know the truth— it only revealed what could never be stolen.

This is the gift.

Chapter 20: Letting Go Without Looking Back

Letting go sounds simple... until it is your turn. People say it like it is easy—"Just move on," "Just forget about it," "Just let it go."

But they do not see the nights you stare at the ceiling replaying every conversation, wondering if you could have done something different. They do not see the way a song, a scent, or a random street can pull you right back into a memory you wish you could erase.

For me, letting go was not one decision. It was a thousand tiny choices, repeatedly. Choosing not to text him when the loneliness hit. Choosing not to check his social media when I wanted to see if he missed me. Choosing not to keep reading old messages, looking for proof that he once loved me. It was fighting my own mind every day because the heart has a way of romanticizing what broke it.

But I had to tell myself the truth. Yes, there were good moments. Yes, we shared years, memories, and children.

But there were also lies, betrayal, and a slow erosion of the woman I used to be. And no matter how many times I replayed the past, it would never change.

Letting go meant accepting that the closure I wanted would never come. It meant realizing I might never get the apology I deserved. It meant walking away without all the answers and being okay with not knowing.

And the most important part?

It meant not looking back. Because looking back is how you get stuck. It is how you start justifying going back to

When Love Isn't Free

what you prayed to be free from. It is how you forget the nights you cried yourself to sleep, the days you felt invisible, the times you begged for love that should have been given freely.

So, I did not just let him go—I let go of the fantasy, the "what ifs," the version of myself who thought love had to be earned.

Now, when I think about him, it is not with longing. It is with gratitude. Because losing him gave me back *me*.

Chapter 21: When the Strong One Finally Breaks

People think being the "strong one" means you are unshakable.

That nothing gets to you.

That you can take any hit, smile through the pain, and keep going without missing a step.

And for a long time, I played that role perfectly.

I carried everyone else's weight while silently drowning under my own.

I was the go-to. The dependable one. The one who "had it all together."

Ernsie Fidelia

But no one asked if *I* was okay.
No one saw the cracks forming under the surface.

No one noticed that my smile did not reach my eyes anymore.

When the strong one breaks, it is not a quiet fall. It is years of swallowed pain erupting all at once.

It is the tears you have been holding back flooding out so fast you cannot breathe.

It is screaming into a pillow because you cannot let your kids hear. It is lying in bed, staring at the ceiling, wondering if anyone would even notice if you disappeared.

I broke in ways I did not think were possible.

Not just because of him—but because of years of putting myself last. Because I thought my worth was in how much I could endure.

When Love Isn't Free

But here is what I learned in the breaking: Even strong people needed saving.

Even strong people need to put down the weight and rest.

Even strong people have the right to fall apart.

That breakdown was the most painful thing I have ever been through— but it was also the beginning of my breakthrough.

Because when you hit the floor, there has nowhere left to go but up. And this time, when I stood, I stood for *me*.

Chapter 22: The Freedom in Acceptance

Acceptance does not happen all at once.

It is not a single moment where the pain disappears, and everything makes sense.

It is a slow, aching surrender—a realization that no amount of wishing, praying, or holding on will change what is.

For a long time, I fought it.

I replayed the past repeatedly, looking for the moment I could have saved us.

I tried to make sense of why someone I gave my all could look at me like I was disposable.

Ernsie Fidelia

I wanted closure, but what I really wanted was for him to wake up and see my worth.

But the day I truly accepted that he would not—that he *could not* —was the day I started to breathe again.

Acceptance is not about agreeing with what happened.

It is about acknowledging it and deciding it no longer has the power to control you.

It is saying, "Yes, it happened. Yes, it hurt. But no, it will not define me."

The heartbreak did not vanish when I accepted the truth. The nights still got lonely.

The memories still stung.

But slowly, they stopped dictating my every move.

I began to see that what I had been calling "love" was really a transaction—me

When Love Isn't Free

giving all of myself in exchange for scraps of attention, hoping one day he would give me more.

And the price I paid for that acceptance? My peace. My Confidence My Identity.

I am not willing to pay that price anymore. Now, my acceptance is different.

I accept that some people will never love me the way I need to be loved.

I accept that walking away is not failure— it is self-respect.

I accept that my life is mine to build, and I do not need anyone's permission to be happy.

And in that acceptance... there is freedom.

Freedom to create a life that feels like home.

Freedom to love myself in a way that leaves no room for half-hearted love from anyone else.

Freedom to be the woman I was always meant to be.

The old me settled for being chosen.

The new me chooses herself—every single time.

Chapter 23: A Letter to the Queen

Queens,

If you are reading this with tears in your eyes, I want you to know—I have cried those same tears.

The ones that burn because they are not just from sadness, but from exhaustion.

The kind of tears you cry when you are tired of being strong.

Tired of smiling when you are breaking inside.

Tired of giving everything and getting just enough to keep you holding on.

Ernsie Fidelia

I know that weight. I have carried it until my back ached and my spirit bent under the pressure. I have laid in bed staring at the ceiling, asking God why my love was not enough. I have screamed into the silence of an empty room, hoping someone—anyone—would hear me.

If no one has told you yet, hear me now: You are not crazy. You are not imagining the pain. You are not weak for feeling it. And you are not alone.

I know what it is like to choose someone else so many times that you forget what it feels like to choose yourself. I know the guilt that creeps in when you finally say "enough," and the fear of what life will look like without the person you thought you could not live without.

But here is the truth that saved me—and I pray it saves you too: You can survive without them.

You cannot survive without you.

When Love Isn't Free

There is no love worth losing yourself for. No relationship worth dimming your light until you do not even recognize the glow anymore. No man, no friend, no family member worth bleeding dry so they can drink.

And I get it—walking away does not feel strong at first. It feels like failure. It wants to rip your own heart out. It wants to die in slow motion.

But I promise you... one day, you will breathe differently. You will laugh again—not the forced, polite kind of laugh, but the kind that catches you off guard and reminds you you are still alive. You will wake up one morning and realize you did not think about them first thing when you opened your eyes. That day will come, and when it does, you will know—you made it.

And when you do make it, promise me this.

Ernsie Fidelia

You will never again pay the price of acceptance.

Not in pieces of your soul.

Not in nights of sleepless crying.

Not in shrinking yourself to make someone else feel big.

You will never again mistake endurance for love.

You will never again beg to be chosen.

You will never again think you have to be less so someone else can feel like more.

If you take nothing else from my story, take this. You were enough before they saw you. You will be enough after they leave. And you are enough right now— even if you do not believe it yet.

Queens, this world will try to convince you that you must earn love by suffering for it. Do not believe that lie. The crown you

When Love Isn't Free

carry was not placed on your head by man—God Himself placed it there. It is not up for debate. It does not slip because someone else does not see it.

So, lift your chin. Wipe your tears. Adjust your crown. And walk. Even if your knees shake. Even if your heart aches. Even if your voice trembles.

Walk toward the life you deserve. Because you are worth it.

From my heart to yours—I see you.

I hear you.

I was you.

And I promise... you can be free.

With All My Love,

Ernsie

Epilogue: Crowned in the Fire

If you made it to this page, Queen—you have walked every step of my journey with me. You have felt the weight of betrayal, the ache of loss, the heaviness of depression, and the lonely nights when survival felt like the only goal.

But you have also seen the rising. You have seen how rubble can become the foundation. How broken mirrors can still reflect beauty. How a woman buried in grief can still claw her way out of the darkness, breathing, trembling, and still choosing to live.

This book is not just my story. It is a mirror of yours. Not every detail, but the heartbeat—the pain, the survival, the hope—that part belongs to all of us. I wrote these chapters for the girl inside you who thought love would save her. For the woman inside you who felt she had to be strong even when she was breaking. For the Queen inside you who is still waiting for permission to rise.

So let this be your permission slip. To heal. To breathe. To walk away. To rebuild. To live. To love yourself—flaws and all. Because if my crown could survive the fire, so can yours. And when you wear it—not tilted, not hidden, not doubted—but proudly, boldly, unapologetically—you give every woman watching you the courage to do the same.

The end of this book is not the end of you. It is the beginning of a freer, stronger, more radiant life.

It is the beginning of the you who refuses to shrink. The you who walks with her head high. The you who knows her worth is not up for debate.

When Love Isn't Free

So, rise, Queen.

Straighten your crown. Step forward into the world that needs your light. Because your story is not over—it has only just begun.

About the Author

Ernsie Fidelia writes from a place of raw truth, resilience, and unshakable faith. As a woman who has walked through heartbreak, betrayal, and the storms of rebuilding life from the ground up, she refuses to let pain define her. Instead, she transforms it into purpose. *When Love Isn't Free* is not just a book—it is a testimony. Ernsie shares her journey with honesty and courage, pulling back the curtain on what it means to love, lose, and rise again. Her words are a lifeline for women who have felt unworthy, unseen, or broken, reminding them that even in the darkest moments, they are never alone—and they are never without worth.

Through her writing, Ernsie speaks to women everywhere: the mothers, the daughters, the sisters, the survivors. She invites them to reclaim their voices, honor their truth and discover that freedom begins with self-love. When she is not writing, Ernsie pours her strength into raising her daughters, inspiring other women, and building a legacy rooted in faith, healing, and empowerment.

Connect with her on Instagram:

@QueenEFidelia

www.ingramcontent.com/pod-product-compliance
Lightning Source LLC
Chambersburg PA
CBHW032050150426
43194CB00006B/481